MATCH OF THE DAY
ANNUAL 2016

This book belongs to: _____

_____ Age: _____

My favourite team is: _____

My favourite player is: _____

My highlight of 2015 was: _____

_____

WHAT'S INSIDE

WHAT'S INSIDE

WHAT'S ^not INSIDE

My dog is a ninja and he's starting to annoy me!
SAYS **PETER CROUCH**

I've met an alien – and got the slime to prove it!
SAYS **TIM SHERWOOD**

My real name is Ralph and I'm only seven!
SAYS **MARIO BALOTELLI**

I sold my own shadow – and now I regret it!
SAYS **PER MERTESACKER**

I've got a pet mermaid – she lives in my bath!
SAYS **PHIL JONES**

What a year it was, readers!

2015: A YEAR IN REVIEW...
...WITH A MAN CALLED ROO!

So Chelsea won the Premier League and Eden Hazard was PFA Player Of The Year. They won the Capital One Cup, too!

Arsenal won the FA Cup for the second year running!

Man. City's Sergio Aguero won the Golden Boot!

WELCOME
ANOTHER EPIC YEAR!

That was an incredible 12 months of football – and you've come to the right place to celebrate it. So put your feet up, kick back and enjoy your Match Of The Day Annual 2016 – happy reading!

96 pages of footy fun!

Barcelona won the Champions League AND La Liga!

And Raheem Sterling became the most-expensive Englishman ever when he joined Man. City for £49m!

Two English legends – Steven Gerrard and Frank Lampard – waved goodbye to the Premier League to join the MLS!

THE BARC3L

THIS IS THE STORY OF HOW THREE SOUT
MOST PROLIFIC, FEARSOME AND EXPLOSIV

FEATURING...
The unstoppable Uruguayan, the awe-inspiring Argentinian and, not forgetting, the quite brilliant Brazilian!

ONA HITMEN

AMERICANS JOINED FORCES TO FORM THE
ATTACK IN THE HISTORY OF FOOTBALL...

▶▶▶ TURN OVER NOW!

THE BARC3LONA HITMEN

MESSI NEYMAR SUAREZ
IT'S REAL-LIFE FANTASY FOOTBALL

■ **Take the best** player of all time, the planet's most flamboyant frontman and the greatest No.9 in the world and what have you got? You've got an unstoppable attacking unit, that's what! Barca's fantastic three scored a record-breaking 122 goals last season, firing the La Liga giants to an historic, unforgettable treble. Here are the facts and stats behind their incredible 2015!

HOW IT WORKS!

They tore defences to shreds last season, but what's the secret behind Messi, Neymar and Suarez's success?

● Left-footed Messi loves to cut inside from the right wing, play a little give-and-go with Suarez, before unleashing a howitzer of a strike on goal!

● Suarez is a non-stop running machine, darting left and right to create space for both himself and his attacking team-mates!

● Neymar was born to take players on – he runs at defenders in the box. putting them on the back foot and forcing them to make mistakes!

● This won't make pleasant reading for La Liga defenders! Look at those 2014-25 stats!

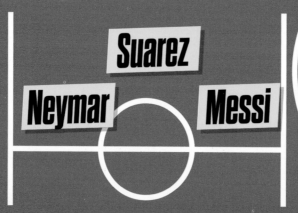

Suarez

Neymar   **Messi**

SUAREZ 25 GOALS

NEYMAR 39 GOALS

MESSI 58 GOALS

% OF GOALS FROM INSIDE AREA

MESSI	91%
NEYMAR	92%
SUAREZ	92%

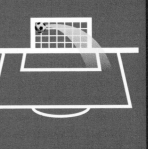

% OF GOALS FROM OUTSIDE AREA

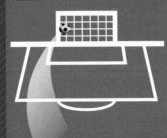

MESSI	9%
NEYMAR	8%
SUAREZ	8%

LA LIGA LEGENDS!

Let's take a closer look at their La Liga stats from last season!

	MESSI	NEYMAR	SUAREZ
MINUTES PLAYED	3,375	2,573	2,180
GOALS	43	22	16
ASSISTS	18	7	14
SUCCESSFUL DRIBBLES	174	104	36
PASS SUCCESS	83%	81%	77%
TOTAL SHOTS	187	95	75

HOW THE GOALS WERE SCORED!

	MESSI	NEYMAR	SUAREZ
RIGHT FOOT	17	30	18
LEFT FOOT	35	5	6
HEADERS	6	4	1

▶▶▶ **TURN OVER FOR MORE!**

THE BARC3LONA HITMEN

MESS!

THE BEST OF ALL TIME

28 years old
He's rewritten the rules of football!

■ Leo is unique in the history of football – the dribbling of a winger, the creativity of a playmaker, the technique of a No.10 and the cold-blooded finishing of an expert striker!

FULL NAME Lionel Andres Messi Cuccittini
DATE OF BIRTH 24 June, 1987
PLACE OF BIRTH Rosario, Argentina
HEIGHT 1.70m (5ft 6in)
WEIGHT 72kg (11st 4lb)

YEARS	TEAM	GAMES/GOALS
2003-05	Barcelona B	22/6
2005-	Barcelona	483/414
2005-	ARGENTINA	103/46

 7 LA LIGA
 4 CHAMPIONS LEAGUE
 3 SPANISH CUP
 3 UEFA SUPER CUP
 6 SPANISH SUPER CUP
 2 FIFA CLUB WORLD CUP

NEYMAR

THE ENTERTAINER

23 years old
The trickster who'll get even better!

■ Fast, tricky, clever and skilful, Neymar loves a one-on-one – his quick feet bamboozle the best defenders on a regular basis, and he's a cool and calm finisher under pressure!

FULL NAME Neymar Da Silva Santos Junior
DATE OF BIRTH 5 February, 1992
PLACE OF BIRTH Sao Paulo, Brazil
HEIGHT 1.74m (5ft 9in)
WEIGHT 68kg (10st 10lb)

YEARS	TEAM	GAMES/GOALS
2009-13	Santos	225/136
2013-	Barcelona	92/54
2010-	BRAZIL	65/44

 1 LA LIGA
 1 CHAMPIONS LEAGUE
 1 SPA... CU...

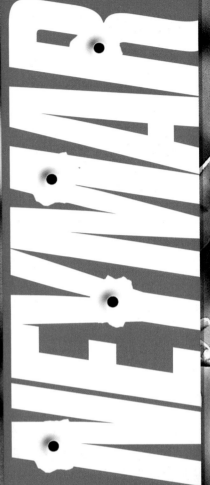

SUAREZ

THE ASSASSIN

28 years old
The best No.9
in world football!

■ Explodes into life in the final third – a twisting, turning, wriggling menace who loves to make goals as well as score them!

FULL NAME Luis Alberto Suarez Diaz
DATE OF BIRTH 24 January, 1987
PLACE OF BIRTH Salto, Uruguay
HEIGHT 1.82m (5ft 10in)
WEIGHT 85kg (13st 5lb)

YEARS	TEAM	GAMES/GOALS
2005-06	Nacional	34/12
2006-07	Groningen	37/15
2007-11	Ajax	159/111
2011-14	Liverpool	133/82
2014-	Barcelona	43/25
2007-	URUGUAY	82/43

1 UEFA SUPER CUP 1 SPANISH SUPER CUP - FIFA CLUB WORLD CUP 1 LA LIGA 1 CHAMPIONS LEAGUE - SPANISH CUP - UEFA SUPER CUP - SPANISH SUPER CUP - FIFA CLUB WORLD CUP

FOOTBALLERS? THEY'RE ALL ANIMALS!

5 HORSES THAT LOOK LIKE NEYMAR!

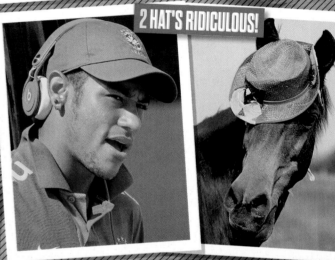
2 HAT'S RIDICULOUS!

1 GOLDILOCKS!

3 HORSE PLAY!

4 ZEBRA CROSSING!

5 MANE MAN!

AN ALPACA THAT LOOKS LIKE DAVID DE GEA!

A SHAR PEI PUPPY THAT LOOKS LIKE DIEGO COSTA!

A PUG THAT LOOKS LIKE KARIM BENZEMA!

Poor old Studge wishes he was as cool as the bear!

AND A BROWN BEAR THAT DANCES LIKE DANIEL STURRIDGE!

MATCH OF THE DAY
2015-16
Superstar!

CR7

REAL MADRID / PORTUGAL / No.7

MOTD PICTURE VAULT

Check out these snaps of footy legends we've unearthed – can you name them all?

You might need mum or dad to help you out!

1

ANSWER

2

ANSWER

3

ANSWER

4

ANSWER

5

ANSWER

6
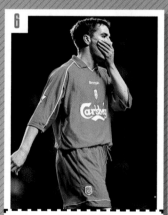
ANSWER

7

ANSWER

8

ANSWER

9

ANSWER

10

ANSWER

11
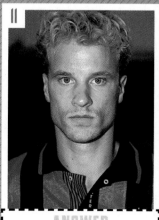
ANSWER

12

ANSWER

Answers on p92!

STAND BACK!

Who's the best free-kick taker in the Premier League? Turn over to find out!

TOP 10
Set-piece specialists!

▶▶▶ TURN OVER FOR OUR DEAD-BALL DEMONS!

10 LEIGHTON BAINES

Everton
The beauty of the Baines free-kick is the variety which, more often than not, can leave keepers beaten, befuddled and bum-down on the turf! His trademark is his left-foot, sidefoot stroke into the near post but he's equally happy leathering it with his laces!

TWO GOOD!
Baines became the fifth Prem player to score two free-kicks in one game, against West Ham in 2013!

9 GYLFI SIGURDSSON

Swansea
Siggy was so efficient with his set-pieces last season, scoring twice from just 11 attempts – the best record in the Prem! One of those, the late strike at home to Arsenal that inspired a sick comeback win, was typical Gylfi – hit hard on the instep with lots of dip and swerve!

WICKED CURL!
In 2013, Sigurdsson scored a mint curling free-kick for Iceland against Slovenia – so much bend!

8 ALEXIS SANCHEZ

THE FOURTH IS WITH YOU!
In his fourth home game for Arsenal he hit a free-kick into the top corner against Southampton!

Arsenal
Sanchez's technique involves scooping his foot under the ball to create height, before crouching his body over the ball to resemble a free-kick-taking crab! It gets the job done though, and creates the sort of ferocious power and speed that keeps keepers awake at night ahead of any visit to the Emirates Stadium!

Man. City
Kolarov must duke it out with another man on our list to take City's set-pieces, but based on last season's results he should get the green light more often. Kolarov scored two in 2014-15, with our fave strike coming against QPR at Loftus Road – a cheeky little dink round the outside of the wall!

MY BALL!
Kolarov had an epic row with Mario Balotelli against Sunderland in 2012 over taking a free-kick!

7 ALEKSANDAR KOLAROV

6 JASON PUNCHEON

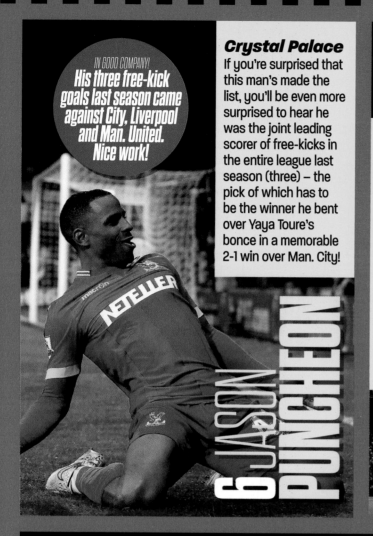

IN GOOD COMPANY!
His three free-kick goals last season came against City, Liverpool and Man. United. Nice work!

Crystal Palace
If you're surprised that this man's made the list, you'll be even more surprised to hear he was the joint leading scorer of free-kicks in the entire league last season (three) – the pick of which has to be the winner he bent over Yaya Toure's bonce in a memorable 2-1 win over Man. City!

5 YAYA TOURE

FROM RUSSIA WITH LOVE!
Yaya scored a sick whipped effort against CSKA Moscow in the Champo League last term!

Man. City
Toure didn't have his most memorable season in a City shirt last term, but he's still one heck of a free-kick taker. The year before he swung home four goals from his first five direct free-kick attempts – a phenomenal conversion rate of 80%! Yaya's thunderbolts are simply unstoppable!

4 CHRISTIAN ERIKSEN

'AVE A GO, SON!
Eriksen had 26 attempts on goal from set-pieces last term — more than any other Prem player!

Tottenham
Eriksen's the only other man in our list who managed three free-kick goals last season. His style is like a high-grade sports car – smooth, fast and luxurious! A master of angles, Eriksen can find the top corner from almost anywhere. Just try not to concede a foul on the edge of the box against Spurs!

▶▶▶ TURN OVER FOR MORE!

JUAN MATA

3

Man. United

If you're looking for a deadly set-piece star, look no further than Man. United playmaker Juan Mata! No other player has a better conversion rate in Prem history – Mata scores roughly one free-kick for every five attempts. With little backlift, Mata punches his left foot through the ball to create a swerve that not many can handle!

2 SEB LARSSON

Sunderland

Larsson JUST pips Mata to second place, partly because he's been whacking in free-kicks since our mums were still making us packed lunches and because he's provided us with some of the most outrageous, gravity-busting strikes of all time! His 30-yard howitzer against Arsenal at the Emirates in 2011 will live long in the memory – it's worth hunting down online!

MEMPHIS DEPAY

Man. United

He may have only just kicked off his Prem career, but Depay's stats from 2014-15 alone see him parachute straight into our No.1 spot! The 21-year-old Dutchman swept home a startling SEVEN direct free-kicks last season in PSV's title-winning charge. Get ready for a series of absolute sizzlers from the man who is set to be the Prem's next big megastar!

AND ANOTHER!
It appears he knows how to start a season — in his first PSV home game last term, he drilled in two free-kicks in a 6-1 thrashing of Breda!

WHO? WHAT? WHERE?

Study the clues and solve the footy teasers!

1

Hmmm...

What am I?
- You're not allowed to play football without them!
- Players have two of them!
- Sam Weller Widdowson was the first player to wear them in 1874!

ANSWER

2

That's a chin scratcher!

What am I?
- I have to run in a straight line for 90 minutes!
- I wear a shirt, shorts, socks and boots!
- But I'm not a player!

ANSWER

3

I know this one!

What am I?
- The referee uses this!
- First used in Brazil in 2001!
- This is only used when one team has a free-kick!

ANSWER

4

Search me!

Where am I?
- The 2006 World Cup was played in this country!
- Its population is 80 million!
- Top European league the Bundesliga is played here!

ANSWER

5

Is this a trick question?

Who am I?
- I've won the Ballon D'Or four times!
- I've only played for one club!
- I've never won the World Cup!

ANSWER

6

I haven't got a clue!

What am I?
- Just one Premier League team plays in this city!
- It's closer to the capital of Scotland than the capital of England!
- A current MOTD pundit was born here!

ANSWER

7

I just can't figure it out!

Who am I?
- I share the same first name as a famous wizard!
- I scored with a header on my international debut!
- I wear the No.10 shirt!

ANSWER

8

Errrr...

Who am I?
- I've managed the same club for almost 20 years!
- I can speak six languages!
- I've never played or managed internationally!

ANSWER

9

I'm stumped!

What am I?
- I'm 1097cm from the goal!
- Players put the ball on me!
- I'm white!

ANSWER

Answers on p92!

Liverpool / Belgium / No.9

BENTEKE

CAN YOU SPOT THESE 11 THINGS?

DIEGO COSTA'S FAVOURITE TEDDY

LOUIS VAN GAAL

THE NURSERY'S PET HAMSTER

JOSE MOURINHO

WAYNE ROONEY'S DUMMY

DICK ADVOCAAT

A BARCELONA FOOTBALL

ARSENE WENGER

TONY PULIS

RAHEEM STERLING'S TRIKE

ROBERTO MARTINEZ

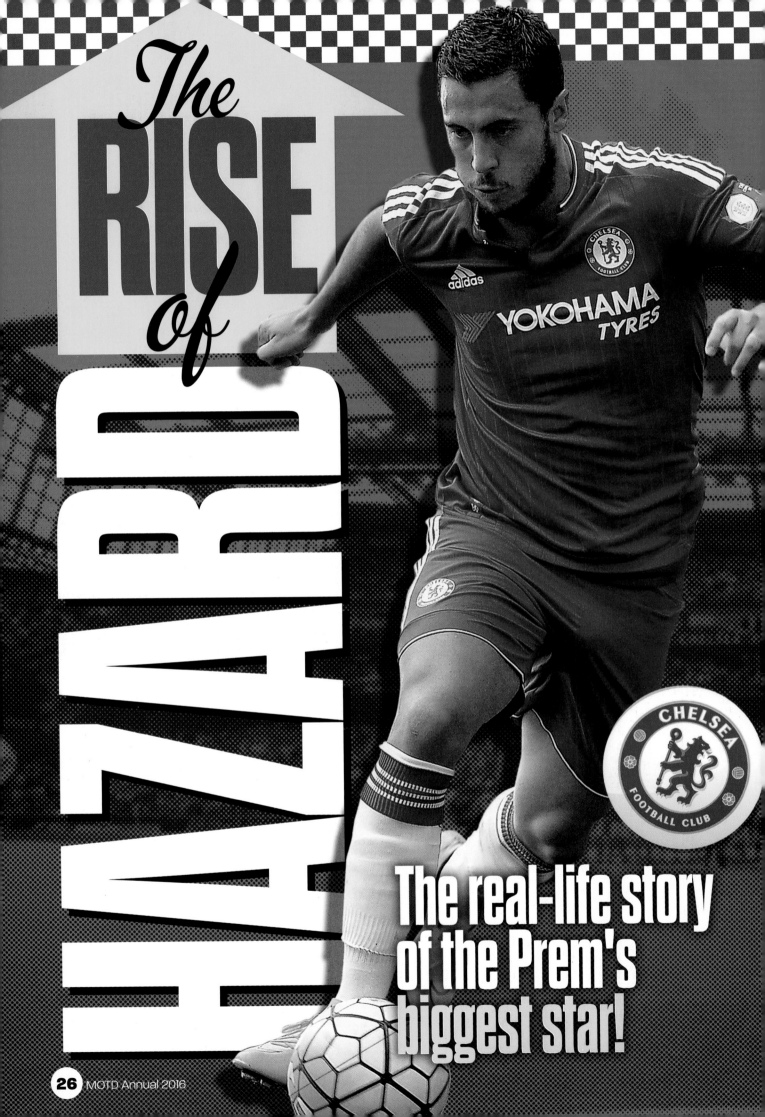

The RISE of HAZARD

The real-life story of the Prem's biggest star!

1991 Eden Michael Hazard was born in 1991 in La Louviere, a city in the west of Belgium!

2003 The Hazard family lived just five metres from a football pitch and all that training paid off as Eden was snapped up by pro club Tulize in 2003!

2005 Just two years later, nearby French big boys Lille came calling and signed Eden on a youth contract having spotted him in a junior tournament!

2007 Eden had to wait two years before seeing first-team action but his debut finally arrived, at 16 years of age, coming on as a sub against Nancy in Ligue 1!

> "We grew up in a house next to a football pitch. It was five metres away, the other side of a little fence. It meant that we didn't mess our own lawn up!
> **EDEN HAZARD**

2011 Not only had Eden now firmly established himself as a starter for Lille, in the 2010-11 season he led them to the Ligue 1 title and was named the Ligue 1 Player Of The Year!

2012 Chelsea eventually won the race for Europe's most-wanted trickster – sealing a £32 million deal to bring the brilliant Belgian to Stamford Bridge!

2015 It wasn't until his third season in England, though, that Eden struck gold – winning the Premier League and PFA Player of The Year awards!

"Last season, yes, Hazard was better than Ronaldo!" **JOSE MOURINHO** *Eden's boss at Chelsea*

"Hazard is a delightful footballer. Breathtakingly incisive!" **GARY LINEKER** *MOTD's main man*

"Can we become European champions at France 2016? Of course we can, but Eden Hazard will have to be at his best!" **VINCENT KOMPANY** *Eden's Belgium captain*

"When he has the ball, you know he's not going to lose it. You know the team has a moment to breathe!" **MARC WILMOTS** *Belgium coach*

"How close were we to signing Hazard? A few millions! Now he's pushing the top two players in the world!" **ARSENE WENGER** *Arsenal manager*

▶▶▶ TURN OVER FOR MORE HAZARD!

HAZARD
humdingers

1

Stamford Bridge, 2012
CHELSEA 8-0 Aston Villa
Hazard picks the ball up on the left, turns the full-back inside out a couple of times, cuts inside on his left and lets rip with a high finish!

2

Britannia Stadium, 2013
Stoke 0-4 CHELSEA
This time Hazard collects a loose ball in the middle of the park before setting off on a driving run and unleashing a left-footed piledriver into the top corner!

MOTD STAT
Hazard made his Belgium debut aged 17 years and 316 days against Luxembourg in 2008!

3

Old Trafford, 2013
Man. United 2-2 CHELSEA
Receiving the ball on the corner of United's box, Hazard jinks back inside full-back Rafael Da Silva and curls a delicious strike inside David De Gea's left-hand post!

4

Stamford Bridge, 2014
CHELSEA 3-0 Newcastle
A wonderful move this one, as Hazard drives into the box, plays a short pass to Samuel Eto'o, who backheels into his path before Eden's clever finish into the corner!

WHO IS THIS GUY?

The 6 need-to-know facts about Eden!

▶ Eden comes from a football family – his dad played semi-professionally in Belgium, while his mum was a striker in the women's first division!

▶ He's one of four brothers, all of whom are pro players! Thorgan plays for Borussia Monchengladbach in Germany and is pretty sick!

▶ He loves dancing, and once stormed the stage at a Didier Drogba charity ball to have a little boogie!

▶ His second-born son is called Leo – perhaps a tribute to the world's greatest player, Barcelona legend Leo Messi?

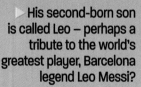

▶ Eden is nuts about basketball! His favourite team are the New York Knicks – although he says he's yet to get to a live game in New York!

▶ The winger once got into hot water by storming out of the stadium during a Belgium match to tuck into a burger!

5

FedEx Field Washington, 2015

CHELSEA 2-2 Barcelona

Hazard spurts into space, executes a brilliant pirouette, keeps the ball glued to his feet, beats another man and, boom, fires one into the bottom corner!

PAZ & BEZ'S

Our lads take over the remote for a weekend

FRIDAY

Hartbeat
7pm BBC One

England keeper Joe Hart is back as motorbike-riding bobby PC Nick Rowan. This week, Claude Greengrass' plan to sell the village church to Qatar backfires, with disastrous results!

Garden Of Eden
7.30pm BBC Two

Green-fingered Belgian Eden Hazard faces a race against time to get his geraniums in tip-top condition for the annual Chelsea Flower Show. Last in series!

Panorama: The Schweinsteiger Who Came To Tea
8pm BBC One

Retired couple Ernest and Edna Dumpty speak exclusively to the BBC about the time Bastian Schweinsteiger turned up on their doorstep with a packet of crispy pancakes and some microwave chips!

Sun, Sea And Suspicious Gaffers
9pm BBC Three

Liverpool trio Kolo Toure, Martin Skrtel and James Milner embark on their first lads' holiday to Rhyl, promising nothing but carnage. But little do they know that Reds boss Brendan Rodgers is secretly watching their every move!

Rattlesnake Roolette
10pm BBC One

Wayne Rooney's BAFTA-winning gameshow. This week Doris Winterbottom comes face to face with a Southern Ridge-nosed Rattlesnake. Contains scenes some viewers may find upsetting!

GOGGLEBOX!

of unmissable (and totally made up) telly!

SATURDAY

My Little Bony
8am CBBC

The Little Bonys are frolicking in their magical Paradise Estate, when suddenly Little Wilfried is attacked by a gang of goblins from under the bridge. Parental guidance recommended!

Petr Rabbit: The Tale Of The Frightfully Painful Stomach
9am CBBC

Woodland critter, and part-time Arsenal keeper, Petr Cech wakes up with a dicky tummy – and suspicion instantly turns to Tommy Brock's new burger van!

Ash In The Attic
11am BBC One

Man. United winger Ashley Young pops round to Marouane Fellaini's house to tidy his loft. He is shocked, saddened and somewhat traumatised at what he finds. Last in series!

Trumpety Trump
2pm BBC One

Tony Pulis hosts a new series of the smash-hit gameshow that gives contestants the chance to win a trip to Flamingo World in Torquay!

LVG & His HGV
4pm BBC Three

Man. United's big Dutchman has 36 hours to deliver a lorry-load of natterjack toads to Warsaw Zoo in Poland. But some unexpected fisticuffs with an angry French farmer puts his mission in jeopardy!

Blimey O'Reilly
7pm BBC Two

Sunderland defender John O'Shea is back as Ireland's much-loved, bungling detective Blimey O'Reilly!

FILM Mrs Dowdfire
8pm BBC One

Disgruntled referee Phil Dowd takes on a second job as a frumpy female housekeeper – but can he keep it secret from his boss Mike Riley? A family classic!

Wenger Jenga
11pm BBC Four

Live uninterrupted coverage of Arsene Wenger's attempt to break the world Jenga record by playing non-stop for 48 hours – dressed only in Speedos, clogs and a luminous bowler hat!

SUNDAY

The Jeremy & Kyle Show
10am BBC One

AC Milan's Jeremy Menez and Tottenham right-back Kyle Walker return with their explosive talkshow. This week it features Tyler from Kent, who says: "My dad eats raw sausages and that ain't right!"

The Great British Badger Wash
11am BBC One

Roy Hodgson and Danny Welbeck take to the Shropshire countryside armed with wet wipes and Fairy liquid. How many badgers can they spruce up in the seven hours?

Fox In The Box
1.30pm BBC Two

Nott'm Forest defender Danny Fox is blindfolded, sellotaped into a cardboard box and tossed into the River Trent. Can he punch his way out?

Kaboul In A China Shop
4pm BBC Two

It's bedlam in the pottery department of John Lewis on Oxford Street as Sunderland defender Younes Kaboul goes ballistic with a rolling pin!

Gotta Be Krul To Be Kind
5pm BBC One

Newcastle's Dutch keeper Tim Krul waves goodbye to his luxury lifestyle and opens a hostel for homeless rabbits. But the sighting of a rabbit pie cookbook on Tim's desk raises suspicion among the hostel staff!

Adam's Apple
7.30pm BBC Two

In this gritty northern drama, Charlie Adam is a lonely simpleton who's lost his job, pet kestrel and all hope – but one day he opens a packet of reduced-price Granny Smith apples and his life changes. Also starring Timothy Spall!

FILM Fuddy Duddy John Ruddy
9.30pm BBC One

The keeper plays a cranky pensioner whose secret life as a swashbuckling hero keeps Norwich's streets clear of aliens, zombies and Ipswich fans!

Cheese & Busquets
11pm BBC Four

Late-night session of 80s classics round Sergio Busquets' house. The midfielder-turned-DJ goes back-to-back with Bryan Robson and Harry Redknapp!

8 FOOTY MASCOTS

THAT'LL FREAK YOU OUT!

George The Gorilla
PERTH GLORY | Australia | **2014**

What do you mean, you've never seen an orange monkey with purple hair before? You've just obviously not ventured out to Western Australia! This Aussie ape looks a bit too shady for our liking, with his fake smile, his fake tan and his fake handshake, he's definitely one scary beast to avoid!

01

YEOVIL TOWN F.C.

02

Jolly Green Giant
YEOVIL | England | **2009**

He may be green and he may be a giant, but there's nothing jolly about this big freakoid! The Glovers must have found him in the local house of horrors because this guy's got a face that only a mother could love! That sinister smile gives us the creeps – and just WHAT is he hiding under that huge hat? Stay away from us, you big monster!

Growler
HUDDERSFIELD England | **2000**

Growler is, quite simply, one of the most incredible creatures we've ever seen! He's some sort of dog, but one that's probably been living in a dustbin for the past decade, feeding on discarded kebabs and bathing in stinky bin juice! In fact, we can smell you from here, Growler, you manky mutt. Have a wash!

03

07

04

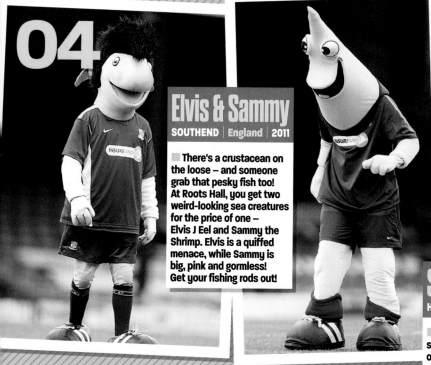

Elvis & Sammy
SOUTHEND | England | 2011

There's a crustacean on the loose – and someone grab that pesky fish too! At Roots Hall, you get two weird-looking sea creatures for the price of one – Elvis J Eel and Sammy the Shrimp. Elvis is a quiffed menace, while Sammy is big, pink and gormless! Get your fishing rods out!

05

Stolle
HOLSTEIN KIEL | Germany | 2014

Apart from dropping off newborn babies, storks don't do much, do they? But this one, from northern Germany, looks like he'd squawk your head off and peck at your face until he was dragged away by his own team of minders. It's the manic eyes!

Zampa The Lion
MILLWALL | England | 1956

If you were to clamber into the dusty loft of an old haunted house, this is probably what would greet you – hiding in the corner, covered in fleas and chewing an old bat! In fact, you wouldn't be surprised to see this fella crop up in a black and white horror movie!

06

08

Mighty Mariner
GRIMSBY | England | 2015

We're not sure what's so mighty about an old pensioner in a sailor's cap, but that must be the way things are done on England's blustery east coast! We've seen more muscle on a mop – but in fairness to this chap, that is a mighty snout! Even Zlatan Ibrahimovic and Pinocchio would be proud of that huge hooter!

Cozmo
LA GALAXY | USA | 2004

We have no idea what this furry green critter is! At first we thought it was some kind of startled frog, or perhaps some kind of extremely rare eyebrowed newt – but apparently his spaceship crash-landed in California 12 years ago and he was immediately signed up by The Galaxy as their official mascot. Americans are very weird!

JUVENTUS /
FRANCE / No.10

POGBA

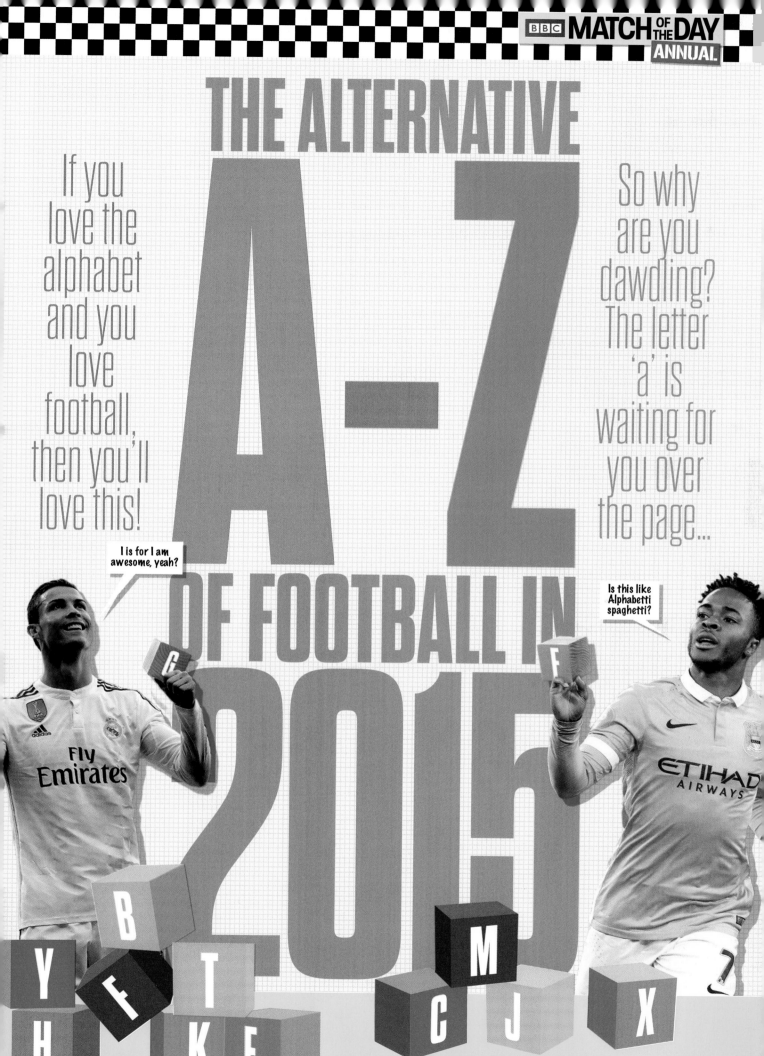

A is for...
Argentinians on the loose

■ You couldn't move in 2015 without bumping into an Argentinian. Some were saving their team from relegation (hello, Esteban Cambiasso), while others were slumped on the bench looking for a speedy exit (that's you, Mr Di Maria). But can one of you ask your countryman Leo Messi to join the fun too? Thanks!

GOOD ARGENTINIANS
Sergio Aguero
Pablo Zabaleta
Esteban Cambiasso

BAD ARGENTINIANS
Willy Caballero
Angel Di Maria
Erik Lamela
Julian Speroni
Mauro Zarate
Santiago Vergini
Paulo Gazzaniga
Federico Fernandez
Federico Fazio
Fabricio Coloccini
Emiliano Martinez
Bruno Zuculini

KINDA OKAY ARGENTINIANS
Marcos Rojo
Sergio Romero
Leonardo Ulloa
Claudio Yacob
Martin Demichelis

B is for...
Barcelona-On-Trent

STOKE-ON-TRENT

BARCELONA

■ We don't know what Stoke boss Mark Hughes is telling these lads but whatever it is, it's working. He's managed to convince FOUR of Barcelona's most talented footballers to leave the home of tapas, tiki-taka and tanned beach bods – to set up home in the industrial outpost that is Stoke-on-Trent. Now, we love an oatcake as much as the next man – but come on, Stoke ain't exactly Barcelona!

C is for...
Chingford

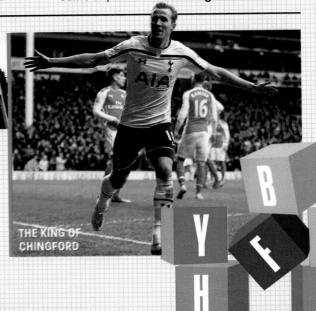

Chingford

THE KING OF CHINGFORD

■ What's so special about this east London suburb, we hear you ask. It's got buses, post boxes and Chinese takeaways, like anywhere else. But it also happens to be the birthplace of 2015's goalscoring sensation, Harry Kane. The Tottenham hotshot started the year with a double against Chelsea and scored 15 more goals before the end of the season!

D is for...
Dick (or Dirk Nicolaas Advocaat, if we're going to be formal)

■ He doesn't look or smell like a superhero – but he saved Sunderland from almost certain relegation. The Black Cats looked doomed until the 67-year-old Dutchman became their gaffer, picking up 12 points from their final eight games to avoid the drop. Dick's had more clubs than golf ace Rory McIlroy – the Sunderland job is his 21st managerial role – but he's still NEVER been relegated!

DICK AS A PLAYER

E is for...
Estadio National, Santiago, Chile

■ This is where Alexis Sanchez etched his name into football's big, fat history book. It was his shootout penalty, a delicately dinked Panenka in front of millions watching around the world, that gave Chile their first ever Copa America trophy. Cool as a cucumber!

F is for...
Forty-nine million pounds

■ When Man. City owner Sheikh Mansour was writing out that cheque for 49 million big ones back in June, even he must have been twitching. It means Raheem Sterling is City's second-biggest-signing, the costliest Englishman in history and the 14th most expensive footballer of all time – no pressure then, Raheem!

TOP 5 MOST EXPENSIVE ENGLISHMEN EVER!

1	Raheem Sterling	£49m	Liverpool to Man. City
2	Andy Carroll	£35m	Newcastle to Liverpool
3	Rio Ferdinand	£30m	Leeds to Man. United
4	Luke Shaw	£30m	Southampton to Man. United
5	Wayne Rooney	£27m	Everton to Man. United

▶▶▶ TURN OVER FOR G-M!

G is for...
Granada, Spain

■ This pretty Spanish town in the foothills of the Sierra Nevada mountains used to be most famous for its sprawling hilltop fortress, which dates back more than 1,000 years. But then in April, Cristiano Ronaldo arrived. He destroyed the La Liga minnows, scoring FIVE in Real's 9-1 win. Ron went onto finish the season with an incredible four hat-tricks in seven games!

H is for...
Hazard, Eden

■ Belgian winger. Plays for Chelsea. PFA Player of the Year. In 2015 he proved that you can try to tackle him, but you probably won't be able to!

I is for...
Istanbul

■ The Turkish capital is the biggest city in Europe – it straddles both Europe and Asia, it's the new home of Robin Van Persie and 2015 marked the ten-year anniversary of the Miracle of Istanbul – the most remarkable Champions League final of all time, which saw Liverpool come back from 3-0 down to beat AC Milan on penalties!

J is for...
Jumbo-sized hot dogs and foam fingers

Back in May we waved goodbye to two genuine Premier League legends – Steven Gerrard and Frank Lampard. After trudging off the pitch for the last time, they dusted off their passports, packed their suitcases and boarded flights to the USA. Now they're playing in stadiums full of hot-dog eating, foam finger-waving 'Mericans!

THINGS DAVID DE GEA COULD SAVE.

K is for...
Kate Winslet

Have you ever seen the film Titanic – the one based on a true story with Kate Winslet, Leonardo DiCaprio and that big ship that sinks? It's a sad, real life story. If only David De Gea had been around in 1912, eh? Judging by his form in 2015, he'd have been able to save it single-handedly!

L is for...
LVG in a DJ

"Hello, hello, hey! Pay attention to the manager," he roared. Man. United's eccentric Dutch boss Louis Van Gaal gave the craziest speech of the year at the club's end-of-season awards bash, which ex-United star Gary Neville described as "one of the best/funniest 20 minutes I've ever had!"

M is for...

Should I stay or should I go?

Making your mind up

Back in the 1980s, the UK used to win Eurovision – no, it's true. And one of the most famous winners was the 1981 entry by a cheesy pop group called Bucks Fizz. Their song was called Making Your Mind Up – which is something Fabian Delph struggled with in July. One minute he was going, the next he was staying. He ultimately signed for Man. City, just hours after he'd insisted he wanted to stay at old club Aston Villa!

X

▶▶▶ TURN OVER FOR N-S!

N is for...
Naughty naughty

■ Look at this chap – it's Victor Sanchez, a defender for Espanyol in Spain. He doesn't look like someone you should be scared of, but don't let that innocent face fool you. Victor picked up more bookings than anyone else last season – including 12 yellows in just 20 games in 2015! Opposition strikers must absolutely hate lining up against the clumsy chump!

O is for...
Ostrich

■ Nigel Pearson, who was managing Leicester at the time, baffled everyone back in April when he lost the plot with a local journalist. Check out what he said below...

> "I think you are an ostrich. Your head must be in the sand. Is your head in the sand? Are you flexible enough to get your head in the sand? My suspicion would be no!"

P is for...
Panto villain

■ Boo, hiss, boo, hiss! Jose Mourinho's got a rival for the title of No.1 Panto Villain – his own striker, Diego Costa. And to prove it, here are EIGHT pics of Diego Costa being Diego Costa!

Q is for... ¿Qué?

■ Que is Spanish for 'what' – and that's exactly what Spanish fans, pundits and players were screaming when they saw David Moyes' Real Sociedad pull off an incredible victory over Barcelona back in January. Yes, THAT David Moyes! To make it even more incredible, earlier that season, Moyesy had already inspired his side to amazing wins over Real Madrid AND Atletico as well!

R is for... Ronald

■ According to Google, Ronald Koeman is the fourth most famous Ronald in the world, behind ex-USA president Ronald Reagan, Apple co-founder Ronald Wayne and Ronald McDonald, the red-haired clown who loves fast food. But Koeman IS the only Dutch Ronald to have managed in the Premier League – and what a bloomin' good job he did in his first season!

S is for... Selfies overload

■ 2015 was the year the selfie exploded – they were absolutely everywhere – but these are our three favourites, all with a footballing twist!

ORANGUTAN MEETS OX

LUKAKU, POGBA AND DEPAY – COOL CATS

NEYMAR AND INIESTA HAVE GOT IT LICKED

Photos: @neymarjr, @alexoxchamberlain, @memphisdepay

▶▶▶ TURN OVER FOR T-Z!

T is for...
Toothless tiger

■ Once upon a time, Radamel Falcao – a man nicknamed El Tigre, The Tiger, back in his native Colombia – was the most feared striker on the planet. But in 2015 he miraculously lost his magic goal-scoring power!

Hello. I mean ROAR – I'm a tiger!

FROM TIGER TO DONKEY

SEASON	GOALS	GAMES	GAMES PER GOAL
2009-10	34	43	1.2
2010-11	38	42	1.1
2011-12	36	50	1.3
2012-13	34	41	1.2
2013-14	11	19	1.7
2014-15	4	29	7.3

U is for...
Utterly terrifying

■ A big thank you to Scottish club Partick for giving us nightmares. Your new mascot Kingsley is utterly ridiculous, utterly weird and utterly terrifying – and looks a lot like a scary Lisa Simpson!

V is for...
Vanatu 46-0 Micronesia

■ Whenever you're feeling down, just thank your lucky stars you're not the goalkeeper for Micronesia. The small Pacific island nation, 3,000km north of Australia, received some absolute tonkings at the 2015 Pacific Games – conceding 114 goals in THREE games against teams ranked 186th, 196th and 198th in the world (out of 209) by FIFA!

PACIFIC GAMES 2015 RESULTS
Micronesia 0-30 Tahiti
Micronesia 0-38 Fiji
Vanatu 46-0 Micronesia

W is for... Weirdest tattoo of the year

■ It was an eye-catching 2015 for Nathaniel Clyne, what with his £12 million move from Southampton to Liverpool. But it was this photo that really caught our eye. Check out that tattoo – it's a toddler version of Nathaniel, in his pants, holding a football!

X is for... X Factor

What do you think, Simon?

■ We're pretty sure Alan Pardew isn't going to be the nation's next singing sensation but he certainly had the X Factor at Selhurst Park in 2015. When he took over in January, Crystal Palace were in the relegation zone – but he guided them to win after win and a top-half finish!

DID YOU KNOW?
● Last season, Pardew had a higher win percentage than Louis Van Gaal and Manuel Pellegrini!
● Palace would have finished SIXTH if the season started when he took over!

Y is for... Yaya happy face, Yaya sad face

■ Yaya's club team Man. City might have lost their Premier League crown to Chelsea in 2015, but his Ivory Coast side won their first Africa Cup Of Nations for 23 years! Ah, well – you win some, you lose some, eh Yaya!

Z is for... Zillion-to-one

■ League 1 Bradford winning 4-2 against top-of-the-Prem Chelsea at Stamford Bridge after being 2-0 down is NEVER going to happen. It's impossible. It's a zillion to one shot. But remarkably it DID happen, back in January. That's why you've gotta love the FA Cup!

MATCH OF THE **DAY** ANNUAL

Arsenal
THIERRY HENRY
Explosive French striker and club's record scorer 1999-2007

Aston Villa
GORDON COWANS
Classy English playmaker 1976-1985, 1988-1991, 1993-1994

Bournemouth
TED MACDOUGALL
Prolific and powerful Scottish frontman 1969-1972, 1978-1980

Chelsea
GIANFRANCO ZOLA
Italian genius and free-kick expert 1996-2003

Crystal Palace
IAN WRIGHT
Dynamic and spectacular goalscorer 1985-1991

Everton
DIXIE DEAN
English striker who hit 60 goals in one season 1925-1937

Leicester
GARY LINEKER
Goal poacher started his career with The Foxes 1978-1985

Liverpool
KENNY DALGLISH
Scottish superstar for club and country 1977-1990

Man. City
COLIN BELL
Nimble midfielder known as King Of The Kippax 1966-1979

Man. United
GEORGE BEST
Unstoppable winger from Belfast 1963-1974

YOUR CLUB'S BEST EVER PLAYER

Newcastle
ALAN SHEARER
Record-shattering powerhouse of a striker 1996-2006

Norwich
MARTIN PETERS
England World Cup-winning midfielder 1975-1980

Southampton
MATT LE TISSIER
Saints forward was a magician with the ball 1986-2002

Stoke
STANLEY MATTHEWS
Known as the Wizard Of The Dribble 1932-1947, 1961-1965

Sunderland
CHARLIE BUCHAN
Tricky forward and the club's record scorer 1911-1925

Swansea
IVOR ALLCHURCH
The golden boy of Welsh footy 1947-1958, 1965-1968

Tottenham
DANNY BLANCHFLOWER
Northern Ireland playmaker pulled all the strings 1954-1964

Watford
JOHN BARNES
Entertaining and powerful England winger 1981-1987

West Brom
BRYAN ROBSON
All-action box-to-box midfielder 1974-1981

West Ham
BOBBY MOORE
Stylish, cultured, brilliant centre-back 1958-1974

MATCH OF THE DAY
2015-16
Superstar!
★

Sanchez

Arsenal / Chile / No.17

KINGS OF THE

OH, HELLO. THIS IS OUR HANDY GUIDE TO

NORTH AMERICA

1ST HECTOR HERRERA

Fact file
Club: Porto
Position: Midfielder

Place of birth:
Rosarito Beach, Mexico

Date of birth:
19 April 1990 (age 25)
Mexico games/goals: 31/0

2nd MICHAEL BRADLEY
USA
Toronto FC
Midfielder

3rd CLINT DEMPSEY
USA
Seattle Sounders
Forward

1ST CRISTIANO RONALDO

EU

Fact file
Club: Real Madrid
Position: Forward

Place of birth:
Funchal, Madeira, Portgual

Date of birth:
5 February 1985 (age 30)
Portugal games/goals: 120/55

2nd MANUEL NEUER
Germany
Bayern Munich
Keeper

3rd GARETH BALE
Wales
Real Madrid
Winger

1ST LIONEL MESSI

Fact file
Club: Barcelona
Position: Forward

Place of birth:
Rosario, Argentina

Date of birth:
24 June 1987 (age 28)
Argentina games/goals:
103/46

2nd NEYMAR
Brazil
Barcelona
Forward

3rd LUIS SUAREZ
Uruguay
Barcelona
Forward

SOUTH AMERICA

1ST YAYA TOUR

Fact file
Club: Man. City
Position: Midfielder

Place of birth:
Bouake, Ivory Coast

Date of birth:
13 May 1983 (age 32)
Ivory Coast games/goals:
95/19

2nd YACINE BRAHIMI
Algeria
Porto
Winger

3rd PIERRE-EMERICK AUBAMEYANG
Gabon
B. Dortmund
Forward

CONTINENTS!

EACH CONTINENT'S BEST FOOTBALLER...

ASIA

1ST SON HEUNG-MIN

Fact file

Club: Tottenham
Position: Forward
Place of birth: Chuncheon, South Korea
Date of birth: 8 July 1992 (age 23)
South Korea games/goals: 44/11

2nd SHINJI KAGAWA Japan
B. Dortmund
Midfielder

3rd KI SUNG-YUENG South Korea
Swansea
Midfielder

AUSTRALIA

1ST MILE JEDINAK

Fact file

Club: Crystal Palace
Position: Midfielder
Place of birth: Sydney, Australia
Date of birth: 3 August 1984 (age 31)
Australia games/goals: 59/9

2nd TIM CAHILL Australia
Shanghai Shenhua
Midfielder

3rd MAT RYAN Australia
Valencia
Keeper

AFRICA

PE

CELTIC
SCOTTISH PREM CHAMPIONS

BAYERN MUNICH
BUNDESLIGA CHAMPIONS

BUNDESLIGA

2014-15

BARCLAYS
#SpiritoftheGame

BARCLAYS   BARCLAYS   BARCLAYS   BARCLAYS

CHAMPIONS
2014/15

BARCLAYS   BARCLAYS   BARCLAYS

#SpiritoftheG

CHELSEA
PREMIER LEAGUE CHAMPIONS

BARCLAYS
PREMIER LEA
CHAMPIONS
2014/15

SpiritoftheGame

LEAGUE WINNERS

JUVENTUS
SERIE A CHAMPIONS

PSG
LIGUE 1 CHAMPIONS

BARCELONA
LA LIGA CHAMPIONS

MEMPHIS

MAN. UNITED / HOLLAND / No.7

TOP 20 TIFOS EVER!

Er... what does tifo mean?

Tifo is an Italian word meaning crazy support. Fans organise mass displays to spur on players before kick-off and it looks AMAZING! This all started in Europe but has since spread to the Prem and MLS!

TURN OVER NOW!

BOCHUM FANS

REWIRPOWER STADIUM

GERMANY,
SEPTEMBER 2012

20

FC UNION FANS

STADION AN DER ALTEN FORSTEREI

GERMANY, AUGUST 2014

19

18

ST PAULI FANS

MILLERNTOR STADIUM

GERMANY, OCTOBER 2006

RUSSIA FANS

NATIONAL STADIUM

POLAND, JUNE 2012

17

SEATTLE SOUNDERS FANS
CENTURY LINK FIELD
USA, OCTOBER 2012

16

15

FUERTH FANS
TROLLI ARENA
GERMANY, NOVEMBER 2012

14 AC MILAN FANS
SAN SIRO
ITALY, MARCH 2002

▶▶▶ TURN OVER FOR MORE!

ATLETICO MADRID FANS VICENTE CALDERON

SPAIN, JANUARY 2014

GENOA FANS

STADIO LUIGI FERRARIS

ITALY, FEBRUARY 2014

CELTIC FANS CELTIC PARK

SCOTLAND, FEBRUARY 2013

JUVENTUS FANS

JUVENTUS STADIUM

ITALY, MARCH 2014

09

BAYERN MUNICH FANS

ALLIANZ ARENA

GERMANY, APRIL 2014

MARSEILLE FANS

STADE VELODROME

FRANCE, APRIL 2015

08

07

GALATASARAY FANS

TURK TELEKOM ARENA

TURKEY, OCTOBER 2014

REAL MADRID FANS

BERNABEU

SPAIN, MAY 2015

06

▶▶▶ TURN OVER FOR MORE!

INTER MILAN FANS

SAN SIRO

ITALY, MAY 2012

05

Ti te dominet Milan

04

BRONDBY FANS

BRONDBY STADION

DENMARK, SEPTEMBER 2013

USA FANS

PROVIDENCE PARK

USA, JULY 2013

CLUB

03

EVERYONE HAS SOMETHING

BARCELONA FANS

NOU CAMP

SPAIN, MAY 2015

02

01

BORUSSIA DORTMUND FANS

SIGNAL IDUNA PARK

GERMANY, APRIL 2013

NO TO RACISM   NO TO RACISM   NO TO RACISM   NO TO RACISM   NO TO RACISM   NO

THE TROPHY CABINET QUIZ!

How much do you know about the biggest prizes in footy?

1 Which weighs more — a chihuahua dog or the Champions League trophy?

CHIHUAHUA ☑   CHAMPIONS LEAGUE TROPHY ☑

2 Who has won this trophy the most?

ARSENAL ☑   ASTON VILLA ☑   CHELSEA ☑   MAN. UNITED ☑

3 Which legend has the most Ballon D'Ors in their trophy cabinet?

LIONEL MESSI ☑   CRISTIANO RONALDO ☑
JOHAN CRUYFF ☑   MICHEL PLATINI ☑

4 Name the last nation to get their hands on this trophy!

FRANCE ☑   SPAIN ☑   ENGLAND ☑   GERMANY ☑

5 What top Euro league is this the trophy for?

BUNDESLIGA ☑   SERIE A ☑
LIGUE I ☑   EREDIVISIE ☑

Answers on p92!

BARC

6 Who has never picked up this trophy?

WAYNE ROONEY ☑   LUIS SUAREZ ☑
SERGIO AGUERO ☑   DIMITAR BERBATOV ☑

CHELSEA / SPAIN / No.4

FABREGAS

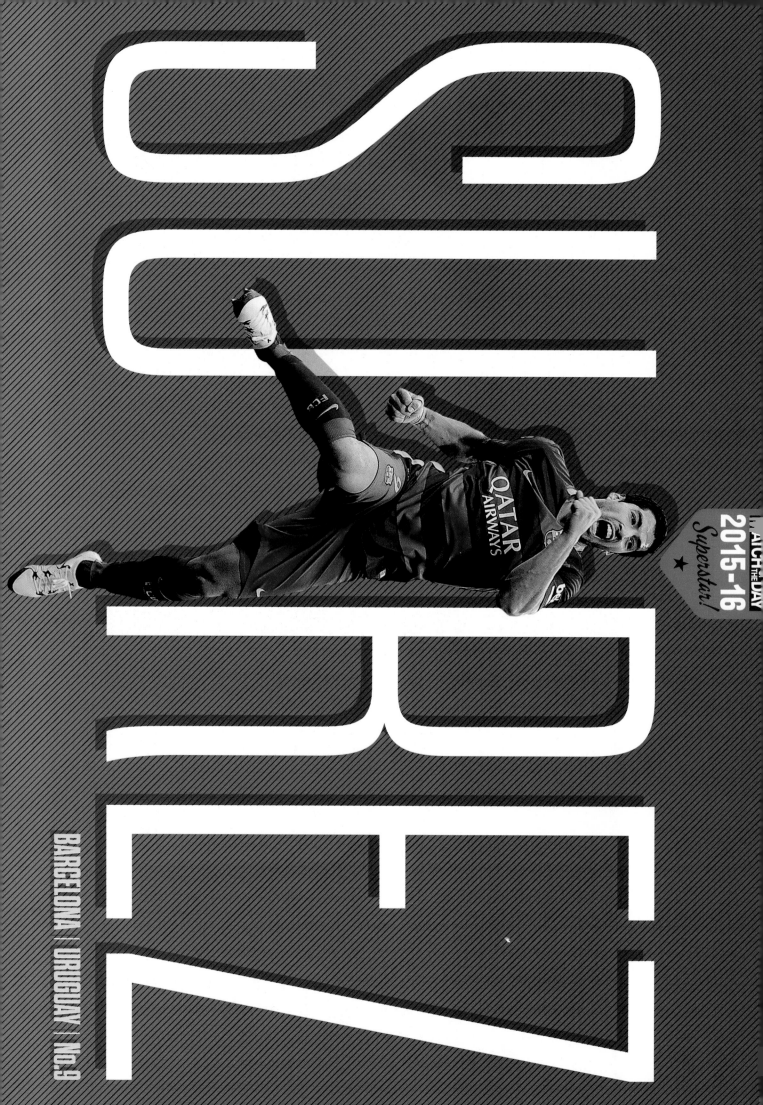

SUÁREZ

BARCELONA | URUGUAY | No.9

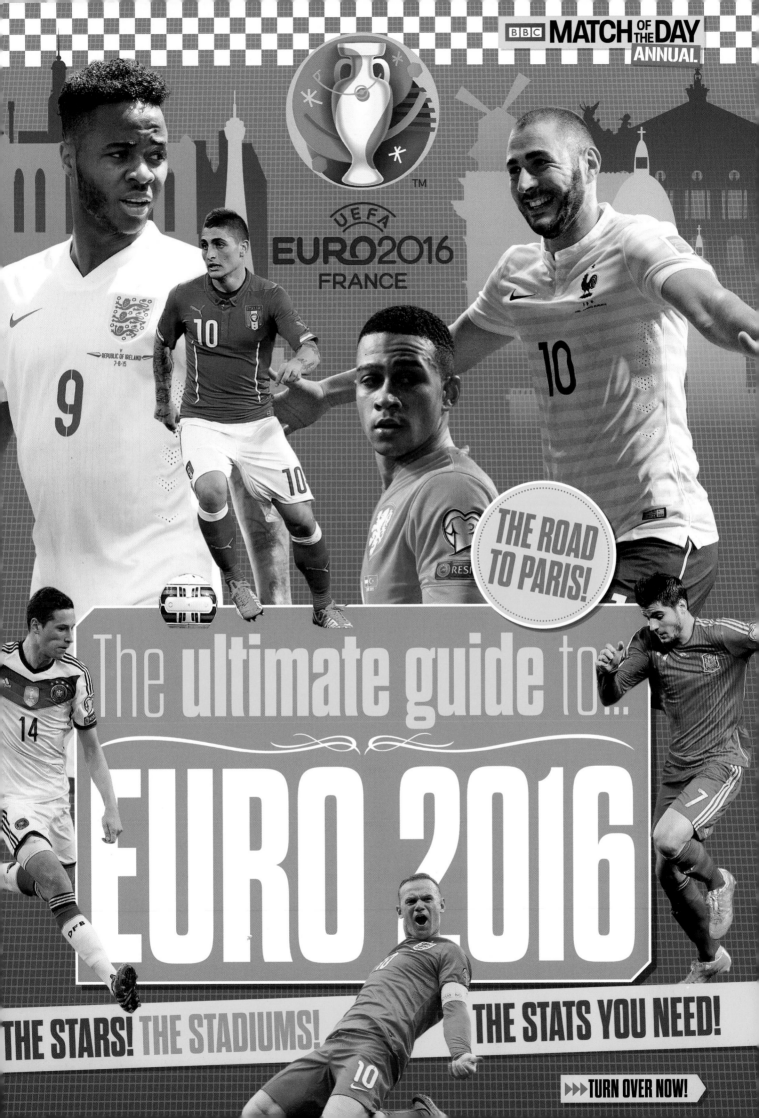

UEFA
EURO 2016
FRANCE
™

THE ROAD TO PARIS!

The ultimate guide to...

EURO 2016

THE STARS! THE STADIUMS!   THE STATS YOU NEED!

▶▶▶ TURN OVER NOW!

6 STARS TO WATCH!

Meet the new generation ready to make their mark!

1 MEMPHIS DEPAY HOLLAND

Age 21 **Club** Man. United
Position Forward

■ Memphis is probably Holland's brightest talent! He was used an an impact sub at the last World Cup but with a season under his belt at Old Trafford, he's set to be one of his country's key men!

Fact of the day
Memphis doesn't muck about – he scored within 20 minutes of his PSV debut and it took him just 24 minutes to score at the 2014 World Cup!

2 RAHEEM STERLING ENGLAND

Age 21 **Club** Man. City
Position Forward

■ Sterling was a risky pick at the 2014 World Cup, but not any more. The £49m man is now one of England's main go-to players. If The Three Lions want to make an impact in France, they'll need him in top form!

Fact of the day
Millions of England fans celebrated a Sterling 'goal' at the World Cup against Italy – turned out it had only hit the side netting. Awkward!

The stadiums in a nutshell!

Stade De France
City Paris
Home of France national team
Holds 80,000
Opened in 1998

Stade Velodrome
City Marseille
Home of Olympique Marseille
Holds 67,000
Opened in 1937

Stade Des Lumieres
City Lyon
Home of Olympique Lyonnais
Holds 58,000
Opened in 2015

Stade Pierre Mauroy
City Lille
Home of Lille OSC
Holds 50,000
Opened in 2012

Parc Des Princes
City Paris
Home of Paris Saint-Germain
Holds 48,000
Opened in 1897

3 KEVIN DE BRUYNE
BELGIUM

Age 24 **Club** Man. City
Position Midfielder

■ This magical Man. City midfielder is approaching Euro 2016 in red-hot form! De Bruyne hit 16 goals and 27 assists for Wolfsburg last season. He's a real attacking menace!

Fact of the day
Kevin signed for Chelsea for £7 million in 2012, but played just three times before being sold to Wolfsburg for more than double the price!

4 MARCO VERRATTI
ITALY

Age 22 **Club** PSG
Position Midfielder

■ If boss Antonio Conte has any sense, he'll sideline Italy legend Andrea Pirlo and let this man take over. Marco's energy and slick passing could be just what the Azzurri need!

Fact of the day
Verratti was an early starter – he's been a regular first-team fixture since the age of 17, first at hometown club Pescara, now at PSG!

5 JULIAN DRAXLER
GERMANY

Age 21 **Club** Wolfsburg
Position Forward

■ Draxler may not start Euro 2016 as first-choice, but he'll be their super sub! Like Mario Gotze, who scored the winner in the 2014 World Cup final from the bench, he's a skilful forward with an eye for goal!

Fact of the day
Draxler signed for Wolfsburg for an estimated £25.5 million just days before the summer window closed in August 2015!

6 ALVARO MORATA
SPAIN

Age 22 **Club** Juventus
Position Striker

■ Diego Costa will start as Spain's lone striker, but his poor injury record means that Morata will get a sniff – and when he gets one of those, the powerful and pacy Juventus striker usually takes it!

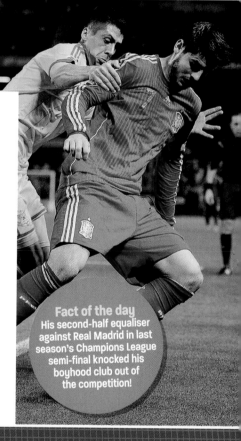

Fact of the day
His second-half equaliser against Real Madrid in last season's Champions League semi-final knocked his boyhood club out of the competition!

Nouveau Stade De Bordeaux
City Bordeaux
Home of Girondins De Bordeaux
Holds 42,000
Opened in 2015

Stade Geoffroy-Guichard
City Saint-Etienne
Home of AS Saint-Etienne
Holds 41,500
Opened in 1931

Allianz Riviera
City Nice
Home of OGC Nice
Holds 36,000
Opened in 2013

Stade Bollaert-Delelis
City Lens
Home of RC Lens
Holds 41,233
Opened in 1933

Stadium De Toulouse
City Toulouse
Home of Toulouse FC
Holds 35,472
Opened in 1938

▶▶▶ **TURN OVER FOR MORE!**

WHO'S GOING TO WIN IT?

MOTD's money is on one of these five!

GERMANY

The current world champions have reached at least the semi-finals in their last six major tournaments and have made the final in three of those! With a squad packed full of attacking talent who know each other inside out, they are strong favourites – and are the team to beat in France!

● Best Euro result: winners (1972, 1980, 1996)

STAR MEN

Manuel Neuer Mesut Ozil Thomas Muller

THE HISTORY
THE RECORDS
THE STATS

3

THREE Both Spain and Germany are tied for most European Championship wins, with both countries nabbing three titles each!

HAT-TRICK? Spain are going for their third straight Euros win in a row after beating Italy 4-0 in 2012 and Germany 1-0 in 2008!

9

NINE European countries have won the title, including Denmark and Greece – but never England!

FRANCE

STAR MEN: Hugo Lloris · Paul Pogba · Karim Benzema

■ Home advantage and a team coming of age at just the right moment means France will be strong contenders! In Raphael Varane, Paul Pogba and Karim Benzema, they have a spine of speed, strength and technical ability!

● Best Euro result: winners (1984 & 2000)

ITALY

STAR MEN: Gianluigi Buffon · Giorgio Chiellini · Marco Verratti

■ The Azzurri's biggest roadblock to success in France is their lack of a settled, world-class striker! Four years ago Mario Balotelli's goals took them to the final, but the chances of him repeating the trick this time look slim!

● Best Euro result: winners (1968)

ENGLAND

STAR MEN: Joe Hart · Raheem Sterling · Wayne Rooney

■ If Roy Hodgson can get just two or three of his young attacking prodigies combining together, England could be a dangerous force. Raheem Sterling, Jack Wilshere, Ross Barkley – it's time to step up and deliver the goods!

● Best Euro result: semi-finals (1996)

BELGIUM

STAR MEN: Thibaut Courtois · Vincent Kompany · Eden Hazard

■ Every man and his dog is tipping Belgium to do well in France, but it would still be a shock if they went all the way. Tactics have let them down in the past, but the skill of Eden Hazard could take them into the latter stages!

● Best Euro result: runners-up (1980)

509
In 2012, Spain went a marathon 509 minutes without conceding a goal in the tournament!

RONALDO 7

CRISTIANO RONALDO is the youngest player to appear in a European Championship final. He was 19 years and 150 days in 2004!

French football legend – and current UEFA president – Michel Platini holds the record for most goals scored in a tournament, with nine in 1984!

KNOW YOUR EUROS!

Piece together the clues and work out which Euro nation we're on about!

NATION 1

FAMOUS FOOD

RECENT EUROS RECORD
- 2012 Quarter-finals
- 2008 Group stage
- 2004 Quarter-finals
- 2000 Champions

MOST CAPPED PLAYER

LANDMARK

ANSWER

NATION 2

FAMOUS FOOD

RECENT EUROS RECORD
- 2012 Did not qualify
- 2008 Did not qualify
- 2004 Did not qualify
- 2000 Did not qualify

MOST CAPPED PLAYER

LANDMARK

ANSWER

NATION 3

FAMOUS FOOD

RECENT EUROS RECORD
- 2012 Group stage
- 2008 Quarter-finals
- 2004 Semi-finals
- 2000 Semi-finals

MOST CAPPED PLAYER

LANDMARK

ANSWER

NATION 4

FAMOUS FOOD

RECENT EUROS RECORD
- 2012 Semi-finals
- 2008 Runners-up
- 2004 Group stage
- 2000 Group stage

MOST CAPPED PLAYER

LANDMARK

ANSWER

Answers on p92!

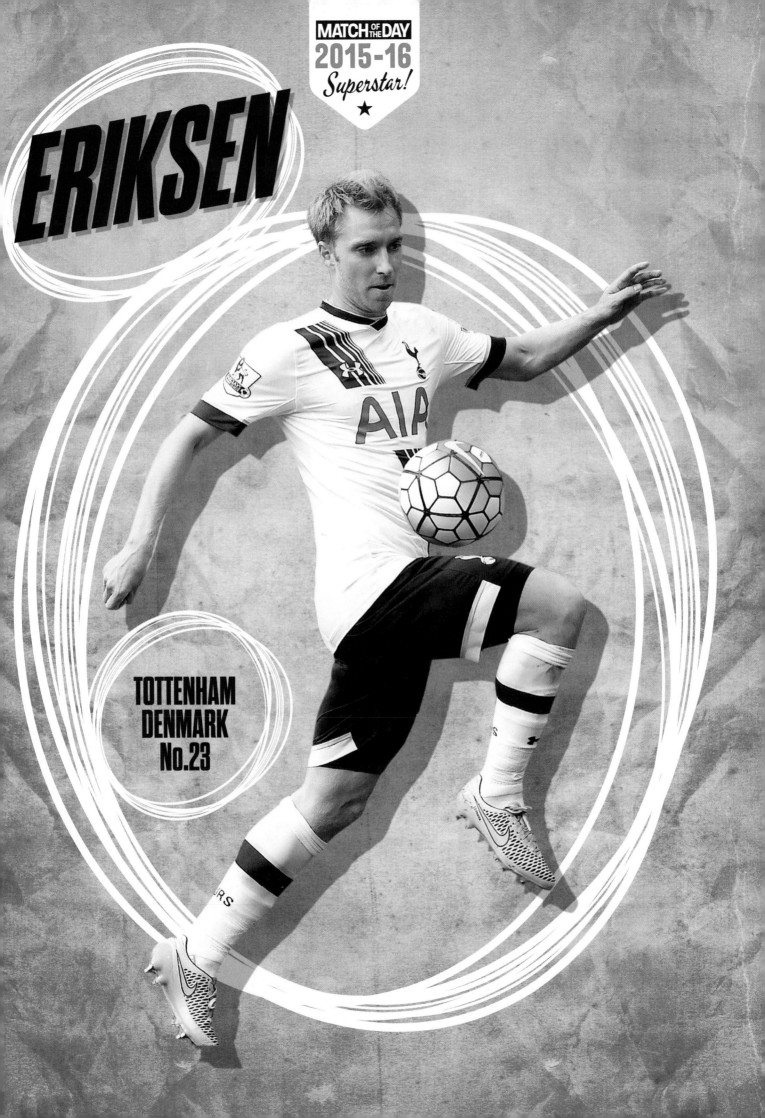

8 Best cities
TO PLAY FOOTBALL IN!
Imagine strutting your stuff in these incredible tourist hotspots...

ROME
Country: Italy
Population: 2.6 million
Clubs: Lazio & Roma

If you like stunning spectacles and ancient history, the Eternal City will be right up your strada! Home of the Spanish Steps, Trevi Fountain and the Coliseum, where Roman gladiators used to duke it out in front of thousands, plus two of Serie A's most famous clubs, what's not to like?

01

02

MADRID
Country: Spain
Population: 3.2 million **Clubs:** Atletico Madrid, Real Madrid, Rayo Vallecano

Probably the most successful city in European footy in the last few years, with both Real and Atletico claiming the La Liga title since 2012, but it's not just about football. Stunning museums and art galleries, epic palaces and delicious cured meats all combine to make this a must-see city!

04

RIO DE JANEIRO
Country: Brazil
Population: 6.32 million **Clubs:** Botafogo, Flamengo, Fluminense, Vasco Da Gama

In some ways, Rio feels like the unofficial home of football. It's hosted the World Cup final twice at the Maracana – one of the most famous stadiums ever built! Off the pitch it has a 24-hour carnival atmosphere, exotic animals to check out, rainforests to trek through and sick samba music!

03

SAN SEBASTIAN
Country: Spain
Population: 186,000
Clubs: Real Sociedad

Here's one for you chilled-out types. Located in the Basque country, the city sits on the north coast of Spain in the Bay Of Biscay, with perfect conditions for surfing and delicious pinchos – the Basque answer to tapas. The only drawback here is being managed by David Moyes!

05

LONDON

Country: England
Population: 8.3 million
Clubs: Arsenal, Chelsea, Crystal Palace, Tottenham, West Ham

London boasts a rich footballing heritage, home to no fewer than five current top-flight clubs who have won the title 18 times between them! The setting for English football's greatest triumph – the 1966 World Cup win over West Germany at the old Wembley Stadium – London is one of the few cities in the world where you can hear over 300 languages on the street and also visit Henry VIII's old gaff!

06

BUENOS AIRES

Country: Argentina
Population: 2.9 million **Clubs:** Boca Juniors, River Plate, San Lorenzo, Velez Sarsfield

Portenos – as the residents are known in Buenos Aires – don't just like football, they absolutely flipping adore it. This makes for some of the most fiery encounters in world football, especially the derby between the country's most famous clubs – Boca Juniors and River Plate! Win that and you'll walk the streets a hero, lose and it'll be no tango for you – you won't want to leave the house!

VIENNA

Country: Austria
Population: 1.7 million
Clubs: Rapid Vienna, Austria Vienna

Between 1978 and 1988, the Austrian Bundesliga title went to a team from Vienna 11 times in a row! The clubs from the capital have fallen on harder times in recent years but that doesn't take away from the city's incredible architecture, fantastic classical music and the fact that, this year, for the sixth time in a row, it was voted the world's happiest city!

07

NEW YORK

Country: USA
Population: 8.4 million
Clubs: New York Red Bulls, New York City

If it's good enough for Frank Lampard, it's good enough for us! While the standard of football is still getting up to scratch, there's nothing second-rate about Manhattan, the city that never sleeps, according to Frank Sinatra. Huge sandwiches, even bigger skyscrapers and some of the best theatre in the world are all available from dawn till dusk!

08

MAN. CITY | **ARGENTINA** | **No.10**

RIDICULOUS SICKULOUS FOOTY RHYMES!

Poetry? Are you havin' a laugh?

13 HILARIOUS POEMS GUARANTEED TO TICKLE!

MOTD's book of very funny football verse!

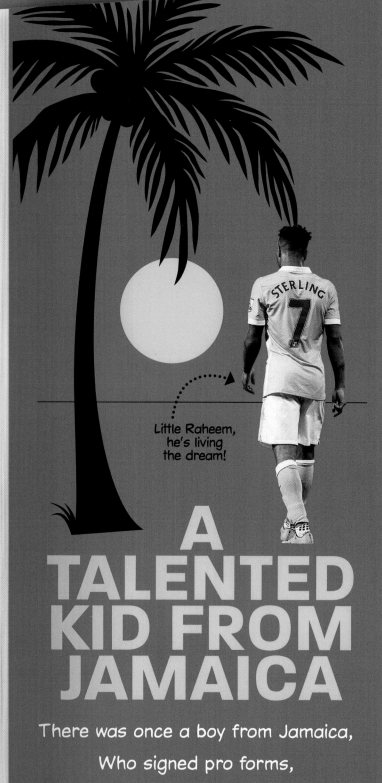

Little Raheem, he's living the dream!

A TALENTED KID FROM JAMAICA

There was once a boy from Jamaica,

Who signed pro forms,

Almost fresh out of day care.

He's a talented kid,

Now worth 50 million quid,

City bosses are praying he'll stay there!

ARGENTINA MUST BE RUBBISH

Argentina must be rubbish,
When you really stop to think.

They finish all these blinkin' finals,
Without a drop of fizz to drink.

They seem to do the hard part,
Then stutter at the last.

They're supposed to be a power,
But they're living in the past.

Spare a thought for Leo Messi,
He's better than the rest.

But on international duty,
His team's always second best!

They come from near and far to watch the fantastical Neymar!

NEYMAR JUNIOR

He came with the name Neymar Junior,
The boy with the quiff and the rings.
Worth a mint, not too skint, Neymar Junior,
He promised such big things.
He played for one term without glory,
Then quickly he came to the fore.
With a kiss, couldn't miss, what a story,
With silverware galore!

WHATEVER HAPPENED TO WAZZA?

Whatever has happened to Wazza,
The teen who could take on them all?

Whatever has happened to Wazza,
The saviour of English football?

Whatever has happened to Wazza,
That freckly, young Mersey Pele?

Whatever has happened to Wazza,
The goal king of Match Of The Day?

Whatever has happened to Wazza,
His passing, his volleys, his skill?

Whatever has happened to Wazza,
The power, the pleasure, the thrill?

We'll tell you what's happened to Wazza,
And all of that fleet-footed gold.

We'll tell you what's happened to Wazza,
To be honest, he's just getting old!

WHAT'S UP SCHLUPP?

What's up Jeffrey Schlupp?
You're looking awful glum.

Has that mean boss Ranieri
Kicked you up the bum?

Has he got you running
From Bangkok to Timbuktu?

Has he banned the toilet
And made you eat cold stew?

Has he shouted sternly
Or pelted you with cod?

Don't you think it's time you tried
To look for a new job?

Too slow, Schlupp! You've got to speed up!

YAYA THE SLEEPING GIANT

We'll tell you the problem with Yaya,

He plays like he's still half asleep.

If he's not in the mood, He's one lazy dude,

And his shooting boots don't get a peep!

TIME FOR TEA

It's time to come in for your tea now,

You can't kick that ball any more!

It's time to come in for your tea now,

Leave those dirty boots by the back door!

It's time to come in for your tea now,

I don't care what Darren's mum said!

It's time to come in for your tea now,

And when that's done – it's straight off to bed!

MR WENGER'S OVERSIZED COAT

Mr Wenger, what is with that coat?
If you pull the cord does that thing float?

Can you blow it up like a big airbed?
Do your feet hang off, does it hurt your head?

Did they have it in a smaller size?
Did you buy it just to warm your thighs?

Would you sell it on for 50 quid?
Would you really miss it if you did?

Mr Wenger, what is with that coat?
We think it's awful. Quote, unquote.

Is that coat just a novelty boat?

SILLY OLD MOU

What's wrong with you,
You silly old Mou?

You won the Prem last year
But still that won't do.

You're sneering and jeering
All over the place.

Shouldn't you keep your cool
In this hot title race?

The pressure from rivals
Is trouble enough,

Just wait until Easter,
That's when it gets tough.

And if you keep exploding
You know what they'll do.

They'll ban your bum from
the touchline,
You silly old Mou!

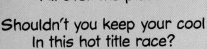

LIFE IN LEAGUE TWO

Would you ever sign
for Leyton Orient?

Way down in the depths
of League Two.

If you've got your own boots
and some shinpads,

They're desperate for
players like you.

They won't pay you millions
and squillions,

There isn't much money at all.

But at the foot of the Football
League pyramid,

At least there's not
a long way to fall.

You shouldn't go there
for the glory,

They're a bit short
on silverware, too.

But it ain't ever boring,
And the fans, they're adoring,

Even if there are sometimes
quite few!

PREMIER LEAGUE

CHAMPIONSHIP

LEAGUE ONE

LEAGUE TWO

GIVE THE BUS A MISS, MATE

Don't ever catch a bus to the game,

Not unless you want to live with the shame,

Of being that poor, lost, old unlucky soul,

Who's gone and missed the opening goal!

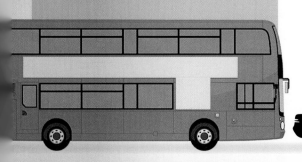

HAVE YOU EVER PLAYED BONGOS WITH NASRI?

The bongo, the bongo, he plays them in the congo!

Have you ever played bongos with Nasri?

We've heard he can rap out a beat.

His rhythm's as grand As a marching brass band,

And he plays them just with his feet!

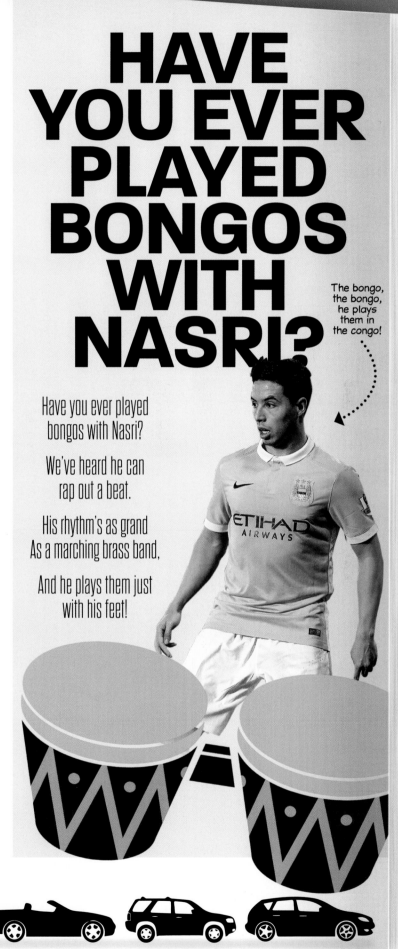

THE HEADCASE KEEPER

Is playing with Per just one big nightmare!

You know that keeper in the rugby headgear,
Has a move to the Emirates ruined his career?
Will The Gunners back four finally drive him crackers?
Will his gaffes be worse than Mertesacker's?
Will he drop them, punch them, lose them, fumble?
Will he get sent in an awkward tumble?
Will the living legend live to rue the day,
Mr Mourinho let him have his way?

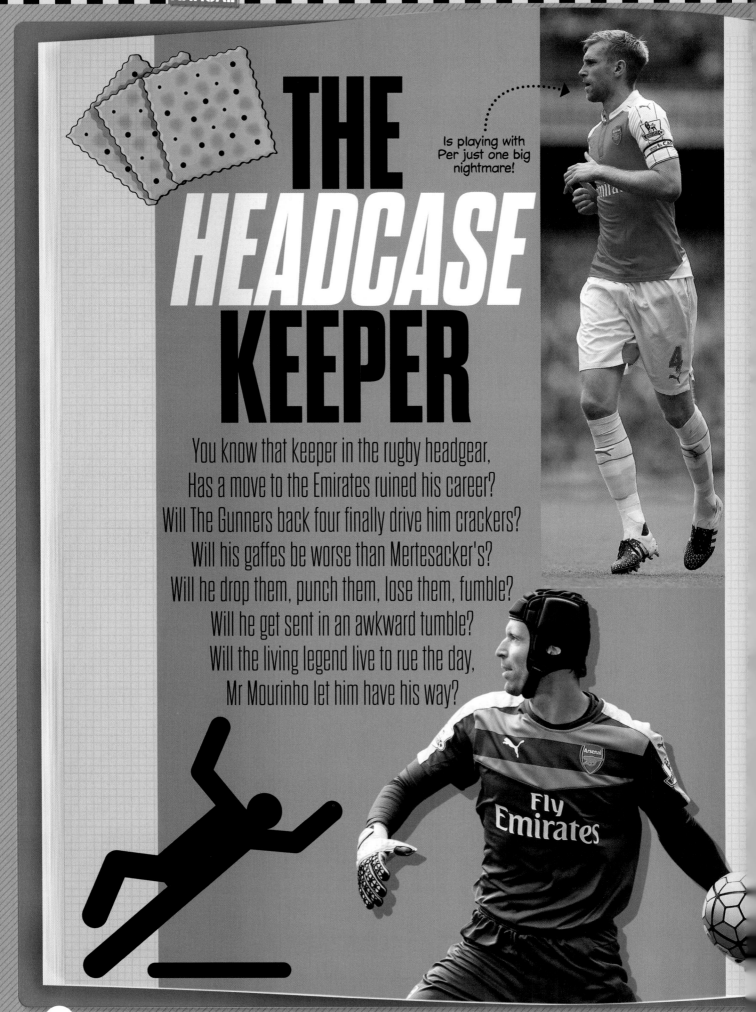

BAR KL EY

Everton / England / No.20

PAZ & BEZ'S...
HOROSCOPES

ARIES
21 MARCH TO 19 APRIL

FAMOUS ARIES
Manuel Neuer

Eek! Your ruling planet Uranus has decamped to Saturn. But don't feel pressured into dressing up as Yaya Toure for that party – it will end in tears. When defending, remember what Taylor Swift said – if in doubt, kick it out!

- **TONIGHT:** Carve the Nou Camp out of mature cheddar!
- **LUCKY PLAYER:** Creedence Clearwater Couto (Santa Cruz, Brazil)
- **LUCKY TEAM:** Mighty Blackpool FC (Sierra Leone)
- **2016 CATCHPHRASE:** You'll have someone's eye out with that!

TAURUS
20 APRIL TO 20 MAY

FAMOUS TAURUS
David Luiz

Yowser! The aligning of Pluto and Netune is a classic astro jackpot. Don't fall for your teacher's mind games – he's not Jose Mourinho. And your life-long obsession with Gabby Agbonlahor is finally going to reap some rewards!

- **TONIGHT:** Lend Marouane Fellaini your bike!
- **LUCKY PLAYER:** Dolly Menga (Tondela, Portugal)
- **LUCKY TEAM:** King Faisal Babes FC (Ghana)
- **2016 CATCHPHRASE:** Sausages, sausages, bring out the sausages!

GEMINI
21 MAY TO 20 JUNE

FAMOUS GEMINI
Sergio Aguero

Oops! Looks like Mercury has entered your solar stream and created more chaos than an up-and-under into the penalty area. Channel your inner Peter Crouch and you'll be okay. A trip to Wembley will be fun – if you enjoy losing!

- **TONIGHT:** Email Brendan Rodgers!
- **LUCKY PLAYER:** Abu Ogogo (Shrewsbury, England)
- **LUCKY TEAM:** Chicken Inn FC (Zimbabwe)
- **2016 CATCHPHRASE:** Let's get ready to rumble!

CANCER
21 JUNE TO 22 JULY

FAMOUS CANCER
Lionel Messi

Lunar whoops! This is going to be a fist-pumping year. A team playing in blue and white will bring you smiles. Avoid back-passes, cocky celebrations and men with big noses – they'll all result in utter embarrassment!

- **TONIGHT:** Make a papier-mache Andros Townsend!
- **LUCKY PLAYER:** Papy Djilobodji (Chelsea, England)
- **LUCKY TEAM:** Insurance Management Bears FC (Bahamas)
- **2016 CATCHPHRASE:** Is this a pork chop I see before me?

LEO
23 JULY TO 22 AUGUST

FAMOUS LEO
Louis Van Gaal

Sheesh! Those pesky Virgos have ruffled your astro-feathers. But don't worry – a surprise meeting with Zlatan Ibrahimovic in Lidl will result in free eggs for life. Ditch the keeper gloves and show the world that you can play. Go get 'em, tiger!

- **TONIGHT:** Slap in a transfer request!
- **LUCKY PLAYER:** Faty Papy (Bidvest Wits, South Africa)
- **LUCKY TEAM:** Happy Valley (Hong Kong)
- **2016 CATCHPHRASE:** How's about you put a sock in it, mate?

VIRGO
23 AUGUST TO 22 SEPTEMBER

FAMOUS VIRGO
Daniel Sturridge

Yikes! Full moons galore over the next year for you, you lucky little sausage. A shinpad will bring you good fortune, but avoid eye contact with Wigan owner Dave Whelan – that will only end in heartbreak!

- **TONIGHT:** Conduct a scientific experiment on Everton's Tony Hibbert!
- **LUCKY PLAYER:** Surprise Moriri (Mamelodi Sundowns, South Africa)
- **LUCKY TEAM:** Army United (Thailand)
- **2016 CATCHPHRASE:** Don't touch what you can't afford!

2016!

If you believe these, you'll believe anything!

It's astrological nonsense!

LIBRA

23 SEPTEMBER TO 22 OCTOBER

FAMOUS LIBRA:
Diego Costa

Whoosh! Jupiter has floated into your cosmic garden and we all know what that means – a hug from Steve McClaren is coming your way in the next 12 months. Resist temptation to slide tackle that annoying woman next door – she'll retaliate with gusto!

- TONIGHT: Tell everyone that Dwight Gayle is your brother!
- LUCKY PLAYER: Boubacar Barry (Lokeren, Belgium)
- LUCKY TEAM: Dandy Town Hornets (Bermuda)
- 2016 CATCHPHRASE: I'm kind of a big deal round here!

SCORPIO

23 OCTOBER TO 22 NOVEMBER

FAMOUS SCORPIO
Wayne Rooney

Beware! This is a period of cosmic upheaval, so be ready for that. That dream about Sam Allardyce, the camel and the Arabian prince will suddenly make sense. Avoid aerial challenges and horseplay with Christian Benteke!

- TONIGHT: Run for the FIFA presidency!
- LUCKY PLAYER: Mario Eggimann (FC Union Berlin, Germany)
- LUCKY TEAM: The Strongest (Bolivia)
- 2016 CATCHPHRASE: This is no time for tomfoolery!

SAGITTARIUS

23 NOVEMBER TO 18 DECEMBER

FAMOUS SAGITTARIUS
Raheem Sterling

Woah! A cosmic cyclone blows stardust into your astro-eyes in 2016. A doddery old man called Roy will confuse you. Don't throw away those footy socks – they'll rescue you from a fate worse than death next summer!

- TONIGHT: Put that cap on and strut like you're Tony Pulis!
- LUCKY PLAYER: Banana Yaya (Platanias, Greece)
- LUCKY TEAM: Ebusua Dwarfs (Ghana)
- 2016 CATCHPHRASE: Your guess is as good as mine, sonny Jim!

CAPRICORN

22 DECEMBER TO 19 JANUARY

FAMOUS CAPRICORN
Eden Hazard

Uh-oh! A full moon is heading your way. Don't let Arsene Wenger pull the wool over your eyes. A discarded pair of Predators will come back to haunt you and a big Dutch manager will become your nemesis in April!

- TONIGHT: Rename your pet Garry Monk!
- LUCKY PLAYER: Dean Gerken (Ipswich, England)
- LUCKY TEAM: Colo Colo (Chile)
- 2016 CATCHPHRASE: You look fabulous, darling – simply divine!

AQUARIUS

20 JANUARY TO 18 FEBRUARY

FAMOUS AQUARIUS
Cristiano Ronaldo

Wow! There's an astrological eclipse for you next year. A chance encounter with Danny Welbeck leads to full-scale war in Colombia, your slippers get eaten by Mario Balotelli and the letter H will surprise you!

- TONIGHT: Give Tim Sherwood a taste of his own medicine!
- LUCKY PLAYER: Hardlife Zvirekwi (CAPS United, Zimbabwe)
- LUCKY TEAM: Young Boys (Switzerland)
- 2016 CATCHPHRASE: Toodle pip, earthlings – my work here is done!

PISCES

19 FEBRUARY TO 20 MARCH

FAMOUS PISCES
Theo Walcott

Crikey! A tropical planet shift will result in a lunar tsunami – leading to a French fusspot midfielder becoming your best friend. A penalty shootout will make you a star but don't accept Rafa Benitez's request – it's not what it seems!

- TONIGHT: Don't dive in, stay on your feet!
- LUCKY PLAYER: Jazzi Barnum-Bobb (Cardiff, Wales)
- LUCKY TEAM: Joe Public FC (Trinidad & Tobago)
- 2016 CATCHPHRASE: What you prattling on about now, Desmond?

MATCH OF THE DAY
2015-16
Superstar!
★

ROBBEN

BAYERN MUNICH

HOLLAND / No.10

THE GREAT, BIG
KNOCKOUT
QUIZ CUP

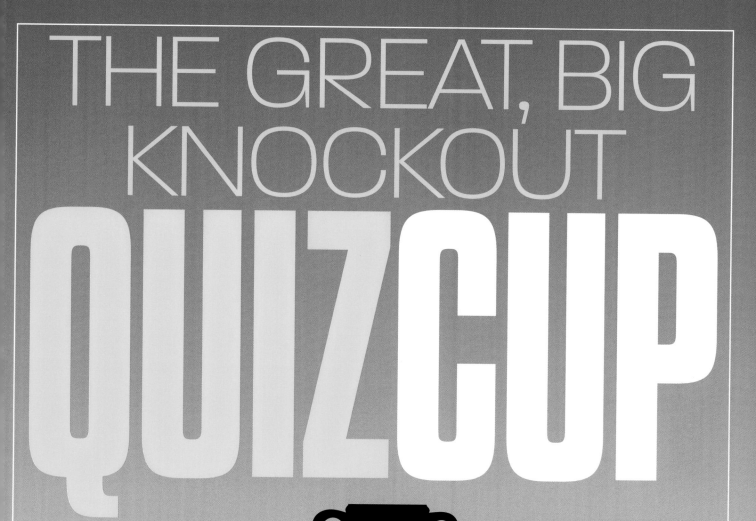

THE AIM OF THE GAME...
Tackle eight rounds of tough footy trivia and you will be crowned our Quiz Cup champion! It won't be easy, questions get harder the closer you get to the final – just like a real cup run! Do you have what it takes?

THE RULES OF THE GAME...
At the end of each round, check the answers on p92 to see if you made it through to the next round. And remember – try not to peak at the answers for the following rounds. That's cheating!

▶▶▶ TURN OVER TO START!

ROUND 1

Q Name EIGHT of England's 2014 World Cup squad!

| ANSWER | ANSWER | ANSWER | ANSWER |
| ANSWER | ANSWER | ANSWER | ANSWER |

Q Tick the SEVEN clubs Zlatan Ibrahimovic has played for from the list below!

ROUND 2

Malmo	☐	Ajax	☑
Juventus	☐	AC Milan	☐
Lyon	☐	Barcelona	☐
Marseille	☐	PSG	☐
Inter Milan	☑	PSV	☐
Real Madrid	☐	Fiorentina	☐
Atletico Madrid	☐	Feyenoord	☐

ROUND 3

Q Match these SIX Barcelona players with the correct facts!

1 Scored the winning goal during extra-time of the 2010 World Cup final!

ANSWER

2 Had spells in the Prem with Liverpool and West Ham before moving to Spain!

ANSWER

3 He was signed from Borussia Monchengladbach for £9.7m in 2014!

ANSWER

4 This South American has won seven La Liga titles at Barcelona!

ANSWER

5 Scorer of Barca's third and final goal in the 2015 Champions League final!

ANSWER

6 He used to play for Man. United but moved back to Barcelona in 2008!

ANSWER

Q We've made FIVE tiny changes to our 350th anniversary cover – can you spot them all?

ROUND 4

Only three rounds separate you from the final, but be warned – things are about to get even tougher!

▶▶▶ TURN OVER FOR ROUND 5!

ROUND 5

These are the FOUR biggest stadiums in the Prem – but can you name them?

1

ANSWER

2

ANSWER

3

ANSWER

4

ANSWER

This lot have all won the Prem title three times – but can you name all THREE?

QUARTER-FINAL

1

ANSWER

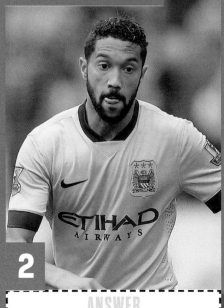

2

ANSWER

3

ANSWER

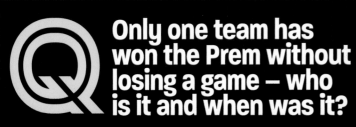

Q

Only one team has won the Prem without losing a game – who is it and when was it?

SEMI-FINAL

Clue! The team was nicknamed The Invincibles after they went unbeaten and this was their form over 38 games — not a single L in sight!

We told you this wasn't gonna be easy!

TEAM [ANSWER] SEASON [ANSWER]

W	W	W	W	D	D	W	W	W	D	W	W	W	D	D	W	D	W
D	W	W	W	W	W	W	W	W	W	W	D	W	D	W	D	D	D	W	W

▶▶▶ **TURN OVER FOR THE FINAL!**

THE GREAT, BIG KNOCKOUT

→ It has all come down to this. Seven rounds of gruelling footy questions have led you to a showcase finale, and just one more question separates you from glory. Can you handle the pressure?

Q Which of these captains has won the most trophies in his career?

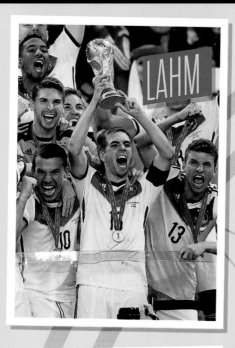
LAHM

KOMPANY

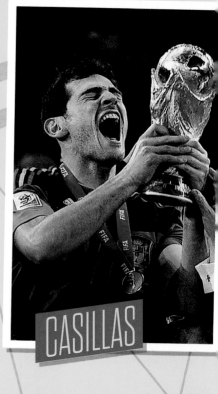
CASILLAS

TERRY

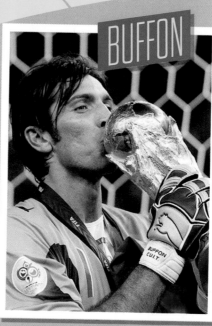
BUFFON

SILVA

QUIZ CUP FINAL

ARTETA

CANNAVARO

KEHL

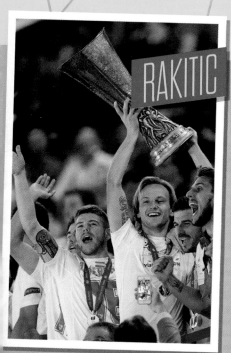

RAKITIC

TOURE

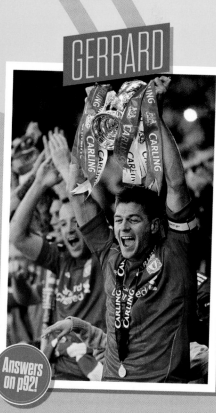

GERRARD

Answers on p92!

ANSWER

Silva

PSG

Brazil / No.2

ANSWERS!

QUIZ 1 FROM PAGE 15
MOTD PICTURE VAULT

1 Ruud Gullit
2 Paul Gascoigne
3 David Beckham
4 Zinedine Zidane
5 Pele
6 Michael Owen
7 Ronaldo
8 Gianfranco Zola
9 Ronaldinho
10 Peter Schmeichel
11 Dennis Bergkamp
12 Edwin Van Der Sar

MY SCORE [ANSWER] OUT OF 12

QUIZ 2 FROM PAGE 22
WHO? WHAT? WHERE?

1 Shin pads
2 An assistant referee
3 Vanishing spray
4 Germany
5 Lionel Messi
6 Newcastle
7 Harry Kane
8 Arsene Wenger
9 A penalty spot

MY SCORE [ANSWER] OUT OF 9

QUIZ 3 FROM PAGE 58
THE TROPHY CABINET QUIZ!

1 Champions League trophy
2 Arsenal
3 Lionel Messi
4 Spain
5 Bundesliga
6 Wayne Rooney

MY SCORE [ANSWER] OUT OF 6

● Did your footy knowledge stand up against our sneaky stadiums puzzler?

QUIZ 4 FROM PAGE 66
KNOW YOUR EUROS!

1 France
2 Wales
3 Holland
4 Germany

MY SCORE [ANSWER] OUT OF 4

QUIZ 5 FROM PAGE 83
THE GREAT, BIG KNOCKOUT QUIZ CUP!

ROUND 1
Eight players from: Joe Hart, Fraser Forster, Ben Foster, Leighton Baines, Gary Cahill, Phil Jagielka, Glen Johnson, Phil Jones, Luke Shaw, Chris Smalling, Ross Barkley, Steven Gerrard, Jordan Henderson, Adam Lallana, Frank Lampard, James Milner, Alex Oxlade-Chamberlain, Raheem Sterling, Jack Wilshere, Rickie Lambert, Wayne Rooney, Daniel Sturridge, Danny Welbeck

ROUND 2
Malmo, Ajax, Juventus, Inter Milan, Barcelona, AC Milan, PSG

ROUND 3
1 Andres Iniesta 2 Javier Mascherano 3 Marc Andre Ter Stegen 4 Lionel Messi 5 Neymar 6 Gerard Pique

ROUND 4

ROUND 5
1 Old Trafford 2 Emirates Stadium, 3 Etihad Stadium 4 St James' Park

QUARTER-FINAL
1 Ricardo Carvalho 2 Gael Clichy 3 Martin Keown

SEMI-FINAL
Arsenal, 2003-04

FINAL
Iker Casillas

● Did you put in the performance of a quiz champ on our trophy teasers?

MATCH OF THE DAY

MAGAZINE

Kane

Aguero

Costa

THE BIGGEST SUPERSTARS EVERY WEEK!

Barkley

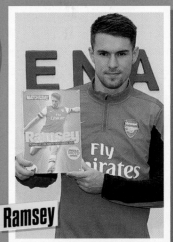

Ramsey

THE UK'S BEST-SELLING FOOTY MAG!

MATCH OF THE DAY

Write to us at
Match Of The Day magazine
Immediate Media, Vineyard
House, 44 Brook Green,
Hammersmith,
London, W6 7BT

Telephone 020 7150 5513
Email shout@motdmag.com
pazandbez@motdmag.com
www.motdmag.com

Match Of The Day editor	Ian Foster
Annual editor	Mark Parry
Art editor	Blue Buxton
Designer	Alastair Parr
Senior features editor	Ed Bearryman
Senior writer / web content editor	Matthew Ketchell
Group picture editor	Natasha Thompson
Picture editor	Jason Timson

Production editor	Neil Queen-Jones
Sub-editor	Joe Shackley
Publishing consultant	Jaynie Bye
Editorial director	Corinna Shaffer
Annual images	Getty Images, PA Photos
Contributers	Ben Hewitt
Thanks to	Gary Lineker, Alan Shearer, Paul Cemmick

n. 02

BBC Books, an imprint of Ebury Publishing, 20 Vauxhall Bridge Road, London SW1V 2SA. BBC Books is part of the Penguin Random House group of companies whose addresses can be found at global.penguinrandomhouse.com. Copyright © Match Of The Day magazine, 2015. First published by BBC Books in 2015. www.eburypublishing.co.uk. A CIP catalogue record for this book is available from the British Library. ISBN 9781849909785 Commissioning editor: Albert DePetrillo; project editor: Grace Paul; production: Phil Spencer. Printed and bound in Italy by Rotolito Lombarda SpA. Penguin Random House is committed to a sustainable future for our business, our readers and our planet. This book is made from Forest Stewardship Council ® certified paper.

The licence to publish this magazine was acquired from BBC Worldwide by Immediate Media Company on 1 November 2011. We remain committed to making a magazine of the highest editorial quality, one that complies with BBC editorial and commercial guidelines and connects with BBC programmes.

Match Of The Day Magazine is is published by Immediate Media Company London Limited, under licence from BBC Worldwide Limited. © Immediate Media Company London Limited, 2015.

2016 FOOTY BINGO!

You don't have to be well old and spend most of your time in the post office to play MOTD's bingo...

The aim of the game: to cross off everything on your bingo card!

The rules of the game: if you see any of this crazy stuff happen in 2016, put a big, fat cross through it, below!

If – and it's a big if – you manage to cross off everything, then you have officially won football. Good luck, bingo brothers!

BOLTON SIGN NEUER, MESSI AND RONALDO!

PLAYER GETS THWACKED BY THE BALL – POW, RIGHT IN THE KISSER!

HUH? ROY HODGSON LEADS ENGLAND TO EURO 2016 GLORY!

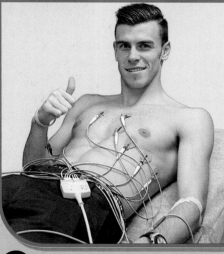

MEDICAL EXPERTS CONFIRM THAT GARETH BALE IS A ROBOT!

LIONEL MESSI POPS INTO YOUR LOCAL NEWSAGENT!